THE
SECRETS
OF
POWERFUL
PEOPLE

H. ALAN MUSHEGAN

ISBN: 0-9755311-9-0
978-0-9755311-9-8

Published by

LIFEBRIDGE
B O O K S
P.O. BOX 49428
CHARLOTTE, NC 28277

Printed in the United States of America.

CONTENTS

BE WILLING TO CHANGE

Powerful men and women are never born that way. They enter this world like everyone else before them—unable to walk, talk or take care of themselves.

Somewhere along their journey, however, they develop the self-image of a leader, one who is ready to take charge and exercise authority and vision.

You may ask, "Aren't people *born* into positions of power and privilege?"

Certainly there are advantages to being raised in a prestigious family, but history is littered with the tragic failures of the sons and daughters of the rich and famous.

For every successful person "born" into power, I'll show you a hundred more who rose from humble beginnings to become prominent figures in government, business, education, religion, medicine, science and the arts:

- Andrew Carnegie was an impoverished Scottish immigrant before earning the title of one of the world's wealthiest men.
- Ronald Regan was born in an apartment above a small bakery in Tampico, Illinois. His family had meager means and he worked his way through college.
- Sam Walton, founder of Wal-Mart, grew up in the Great Depression and helped his family make ends meet by delivering newspapers.
- Noted author, John Grisham, was the son of a construction worker in rural Mississippi.

■ Neither Orville or Wilbur Wright graduated from high school.

The list of those who lifted themselves from small beginnings to spread their wings and fly to lofty heights is long indeed.

What all of these people have in common is that they became dissatisfied with their present circumstances and decided to alter their future.

A DRAMATIC INTERVENTION

In addition to the personal transformation we desire, as children of Almighty God, He plants the seeds of change within us—and often intervenes directly and dramatically in our lives.

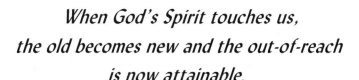

When God's Spirit touches us,
the old becomes new and the out-of-reach
is now attainable.

For example, Moses was not a likely candidate

to eventually be one of the most powerful men in recorded history.

He tended sheep on the back side of the desert for forty years until, through a burning bush, God revealed Himself to Moses—commissioning him to go to Egypt and free the Jews from a 400-year captivity.

Moses questioned, *"Who am I, that I should go to Pharaoh and bring the Israelites out of Egypt?"* (Exodus 3:11).

God assured him, *"I will be with you"* (v.12).

This timid man, became God's appointed vessel—strong enough to stand before a king and demand on behalf of the Lord, "Let my people go!" (Exodus 10:3).

A NEW COUNTENANCE

More than once, Moses, experienced life-changing encounters with Almighty God. When he returned down from the mountain with the two carved tablets of stone containing the Ten

Commandments, the Bible tells us the skin of his face was so radiant, the people *"...were afraid to come near him"* (Exodus 34:30).

_____ ♦ _____

What caused their fear? It was an awesome visitation they had never previously witnessed —the glory of Almighty God.

Moses literally had to place a veil over his face before speaking to the children of Israel (v.35). What an amazing presence!

POWER AND AUTHORITY

Later, when God sent His Son to earth, astounding changes took place in the lives of those who met Jesus.

Following the Upper Room encounter, Peter and John preached the Gospel on the streets of Jerusalem. Thousands were saved and wondrous miracles were happening.

——————— ♦ ———————

*Those who knew these two men
could see the radical turn-around which had
occurred in their lives.*

They were no longer humble fishermen by trade, but fishers of men by divine appointment!

What brought about this difference? The Lord Jesus Christ. As scripture records, *"Now when they saw the boldness of Peter and John, and perceived that they were unlearned and ignorant men, they marvelled; and they took knowledge of them, that they had been with Jesus"* (Acts 4:13 KJV).

They spoke with such power and authority that the Sanhedrin council was confounded. "What are we going to do with these men?" they asked. *"Everybody living in Jerusalem knows they have done an outstanding miracle, and we cannot deny it"* (v.16).

_____ ♥ _____

When the world sees the new you,
they too will be deeply affected.

BOUNTIFUL BLESSINGS

If you make the decision to obey the Lord and follow His commands, He *"...will set you high above all the nations on earth"* (Deuteronomy 28:1).

Scripture details a list of blessings that will *"come on thee, and overtake thee"* (v.2 KJV). In other words, the Lord is going to *chase you down* with favor:

- You will be blessed in the city and in the country (v.3).
- Your children will be blessed (v.4).
- Your land and livestock will be blessed (v.4).
- God will bless your food supplies (v.5) and everything you put your hand to (v.8).

11

- You will be blessed when you come in and when you go out (v.6).
- You will be the head, not the tail; at the top, never at the bottom (v.13).

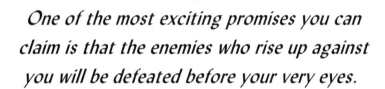

One of the most exciting promises you can claim is that the enemies who rise up against you will be defeated before your very eyes.

The Word declares, *"They will come at you from one direction but flee from you in seven"* (v.7).

Who are the beneficiaries of these blessings? Those who make a choice to *change*—to turn from the sin and indulgences of the world and serve a Holy God.

A New Mind

You may ask, "How can I graduate from where I am to where God wants me to be? What is required of me?"

I believe the answer is found in these words by the apostle Paul: *"And be not conformed to this world: but be ye transformed by the renewing of your mind, that ye may prove what is that good, and acceptable, and perfect, will of God"* (Romans 12:2 KJV).

This verse includes three important factors:

> First: Stop trying to fit in with the world. You'll never be a person of power by following the carnality of the culture.
>
> Second: Renew your mind. Focus and redirect your thought patterns from the natural to the supernatural.
>
> Third: Through prayer, find and follow the will of God for your future and you will know what is "good," "acceptable" and "perfect."

OUT WITH THE OLD!

The moment you see yourself differently, let it be reflected in your behavior.

13

Far too often I meet people who want to take the "mess" of their lives, repackage what they have and suddenly label it "Christian."

Such an approach is like taking the garbage out of one room of your house and dumping it in another, and glibly saying, "It's clean!"

No. The litter and junk is still there—it is just temporarily out of sight.

——————— ♦ ———————

To radically upgrade your house,
you must pull up the carpet, strip
the wallpaper and start over.

This is exactly the major remodeling God expects to take place in your spiritual house. You have to be willing to be changed in your heart, soul and mind. *"Therefore, if anyone is in Christ, he is a new creation; the old has gone, the new has come!"* (2 Corinthians 5:17).

Is it Real?

Don't be shocked if there are people who have

known you for years, yet refuse to accept the "new you."

––––––––––– ♟ –––––––––––

Old opinions are hard to break and it may take time before others recognize what has truly transpired.

This reminds me of two men I heard about who were walking past a taxidermist shop and stopped to look at the display in the window of an owl. Immediately, they began to criticize.

"If he thinks he did a good job on that owl, he's crazy. It isn't even the right color," complained the first man.

His friend agreed and added, "Not only that, his head's too large and his wings are too short. Who is he trying to fool?"

Just as the men started to walk away, the owl turned his head and winked at them!

THE GRASSHOPPER COMPLEX

It's amazing how people can see the same thing and come away with two opposite opinions.

15

This is what happened when Moses sent the twelve "spies" to check out the land of Canaan.

God had already told them to possess the land, but they wanted to know what it was like. Were the people who live there strong or weak? How many were there? Was the ground rocky or fertile? Were the cities unwalled or fortified?

Forty days later, the twelve returned, and ten had a negative report. They stood before Moses and the children of Israel, moaning, *"We can't attack those people; they are stronger than we are"* (Number 14:31). *"The land we explored devours those living in it. All the people we saw there are of great size... We seemed like grasshoppers in our own eyes, and we looked the same to them"* (vv.32-33).

Think of it! Because they viewed themselves as inferior insects, the enemy saw them that way too.

———————— ◆ ————————

If you envision yourself small and insignificant, you will never be disappointed with the outcome.

Remember, you receive what you see!

THE CONSEQUENCES

Just two of the twelve, Joshua and Caleb, delivered a positive report. They said, *"The land we passed through and explored is exceedingly good. If the Lord is pleased with us, he will lead us into that land, a land flowing with milk and honey, and will give it to us"* (Numbers 14:7-8).

———————— ♥ ————————

What account did the children of Israel embrace? You guessed it—the negative word!

This is why God declared, *"...not one of them will ever see the land I promised on oath to their forefathers. No one who has treated me with contempt will ever see it"* (v.23).

Only Joshua, Caleb and their families inherited

the Promised Land.

CHANCE OR STANCE?

If you are tired and weary with the disappointments of this life, believe what is good and step into God's provision.

The man who was crippled from birth (Acts 14) was not dealing with something he lost—rather with what he never enjoyed: the ability to walk. But as Paul was speaking, he looked at the man and *"...saw that he had faith to be healed"* (Acts 14:9).

Here was an individual who didn't know how to walk, yet when Paul said, "Stand to your feet," the Bible says he *"...jumped up and began to walk"* (v.10).

It was not by mere chance he was healed that day; it was by stance! He had the faith to stand and walk!

Change is not the result of random luck or a lottery. It occurs when you are ready for God to touch your circumstances and transform you into the person of power He has purposed before you were born.

Are you ready to boldly step out in faith and walk into His plan?

LOOK FOR A CHALLENGE

I would not be honest if I told you my life had been one of smooth sailing with everything handed to me on a silver platter.

Far from it! The ministry God has allowed us to have today has been forged by prayer, tears, determination, commitment and times of rejoicing.

As I look back, I wouldn't have wanted it any other way. Why? Because a hard-fought victory has far more meaning than simply walking from one easy street to the next.

A COSTLY INHERITANCE

Just because the land of milk and honey was promised to the children of Israel, didn't mean their entry was automatic. If that were the case, there would have been no need for the 40 years of testing in the wilderness. And when the day finally arrived for them to cross the river Jordan, Moses wasn't even there to experience the thrill of this historic event.

Moses summoned Joshua and said to him in the presence of all Israel: *"Be strong and courageous, for you must go with this people into the land that the Lord swore to their forefathers to give them, and you must divide it among them as their inheritance"* (Deuteronomy 31:7).

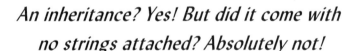

An inheritance? Yes! But did it come with no strings attached? Absolutely not!

FROM DAN TO GILEAD

After informing the people of the battles which still awaited them, Moses went to the top of Mount Nebo where God told him, *"This is the land I promised on oath to Abraham, Isaac and Jacob* when I said, 'I will give it to your descendants.' I have let you see it with your eyes, but you will not cross over into it" (Deuteronomy 34:4).

From this high vantage point, Moses gazed at the territory from Dan to Gilead and as far as the western sea. This was where the children of Israel would soon plant their roots and build their homes.

God welcomed Moses to heaven at the advanced age of 120, yet "...his eyes were not weak nor his strength gone" (v.7).

Now it was Joshua's turn to lead.

THE KEY TO SUCCESS

The Almighty made a vow to Joshua that He would fulfill the promise made to Moses under one condition: "Do not let this Book of the Law depart from your mouth; meditate on it day and night, so that you may be careful to do everything written in it. Then you will be prosperous and successful" (Joshua 1:8).

As we will discover, the Word of God is an essential tool to powerful leadership.

HIDING ON THE ROOF

Before crossing the Jordan, however, Joshua sent two men to check out the city of Jericho. They arrived at the house of a harlot named Rahab. News of the visitors spread to the king and he immediately sent word to the prostitute, *"Bring out the men who came to you and entered your house, because they have come to spy out the whole land"* (Joshua 2:3).

Rahab acted coy and innocent and told the king's guards that at dark, when the gate was about to be closed, the two men left. "If you hurry, you may catch them," she exclaimed.

In truth, however, the woman had taken them to the roof of her home where they were hiding.

Later, she spoke to the two Israelites and said, *"I know that the Lord has given this land to you and that a great fear of you has fallen on us...*"(v.3). Rahab then told them the people had heard how God dried up the waters of the Red Sea when they left Egypt and that several cities were destroyed. Then she made this amazing statement: *"...for the Lord your God is God in heaven above and on the earth below"* (v.11).

THE RED ROPE

Before the two spies left the city, Rahab made them promise that when the Jewish armies invaded, they would show her family mercy: *"...save us from death"* she pleaded (v.13).

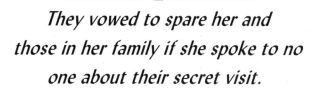

They vowed to spare her and those in her family if she spoke to no one about their secret visit.

Her home was against the city wall, so Rahab hung a long red rope out of her window and the two men climbed down and escaped. Before leaving, however, they asked her to keep the same rope visible so all inside her home would be protected.

PACKING FOR THE PROMISE

Joshua was ready. He gave orders to his captains and leaders to go to all the camps with this urgent message: "Pack your bags!" They were told, "*Three days from now you will cross the Jordan here to go in and take possession of the land the Lord your God is giving you for your own*" (v.11).

The challenge was daunting. Inhabiting the land were the Canaanities, Hittites, Hivites, Perizzites, Girgashites, Amorites, Jebusites—and all the "ites" you can imagine. But even with their combined strength, they were no match for a miracle-working God.

As the tribes of Israel marched toward the Jordan, about a half mile ahead of them were the Levitical priests carrying the Ark of the Covenant.

THE MIRACLE AT JORDAN

When the priests put their feet in the river, a mighty miracle which was foretold to Joshua took place. Even though the Jordan was at flood stage during harvest, the Bible records: *"...the water from upstream stopped flowing. It piled up in a heap a great distance away..."* (v.16). *"The priests who carried the ark of the covenant of the Lord stood firm on dry ground in the middle of the Jordan, while all Israel passed by until the whole nation had completed the crossing on dry ground"* (v.17).

Finally, as the priests bearing the Ark walked up from the banks, the waters rushed in once more.

———————— ♦ ————————

Hallelujah! Their faith was high—
and their feet were dry!

No More Manna

As you can imagine, the details of this miracle spread like wildfire among the Amorite and Canaanite kings of the region. Scripture tells us, *"...their hearts melted and they no longer had the courage to face the Israelites"* (Joshua 5:1).

It is interesting to note that on the day after Passover, the children of Israel started eating bread and roasted grain which came from the abundance of their new land. And from that time forward, the manna stopped falling from heaven (v.12).

Just after this, Joshua looked up and before him was a man standing with his sword drawn. So Joshua stood to his feet, walked up to the warrior and asked, *"Are you for us or for our enemies?"* (v.13).

He answered, *"Neither...but as commander of the army of the Lord I have now come"* (v.14).

———————— ♦ ————————

Joshua fell face down to the ground in reverence, and asked him, "What message does my Lord have for his servant?" (v. 14).

This was God's army commander—and he ordered Joshua, *"Take off your sandals, for the place where you are standing is holy"* (v.15).

A grateful Joshua was more than happy to obey.

THE ORDER TO ADVANCE

The leaders of Jericho heard that the armies of Israel were camped nearby at Gilgal, so they tightly barricaded very entrance to the city— *"No one went out and no one came in"* (Joshua 6:1).

Meanwhile, God spoke to Joshua and told him that, by faith, the city was already delivered into their hands. Then He told Joshua exactly what to do: *"March around the city once with all the armed men. Do this for six days. Have seven priests carry trumpets of rams' horns in front of the ark. On the seventh day, march around the city seven times, with the priests blowing the trumpets. When you hear them sound a long blast on the trumpets, have all the people give a loud shout; then the wall of the city will collapse and the people will go up, every man straight in"* (Joshua 6:3-5).

———————— 🕯 ————————

Joshua relayed these orders to the priests, the army and the people. When he said, "Advance!" they began marching and the trumpets blared.

But Joshua had commanded the people, *"Do not give a war cry, do not raise your voices, do not say a word until the day I tell you to shout. Then shout!"* (v.7).

THE SOUND OF TRIUMPH

Every day, for the next six days, they made one circle around the city and returned to camp.

Then, on day seven, they didn't march around

Jericho just once—but seven times! The priests blew the trumpets and Joshua gave the signal, *"Shout! For the Lord has given you the city!"* (v.16).

The sound of the trumpets and the shouts of the people were so deafening that the walls of the city literally crumbled and fell before them—and the people of Israel walked right in.

What a mighty victory!

A NOTABLE RESCUE

As the city was taken and the people destroyed, Joshua ordered the two men to rescue the woman who had hidden them earlier. Looking for the red rope, they brought out *"...Rahab, her father and mother and brothers and all who belonged to her...and put them in a place outside the camp of Israel"* (v.23).

It is more than noteworthy to read the first chapter of the New Testament and find this same Rahab in the lineage of Christ (Matthew 1:5). She is also included as a woman of faith in Hebrews 11.

———————— 🛆 ————————

*Our God knows what He is doing
—at all times, in all circumstances.*

THE LORD'S ANGER BURNED!

Jericho was not the only challenge for Joshua. There were fierce battles and many harsh lessons to be learned.

At Ai, the Israelites were routed and chased from the city gates. Why? Because one of God's commands to the people—as announced by Joshua—was that none of the gold, precious treasures or "devoted things" were to be personally taken in any battle. They were reserved for the Lord's use.

This directive was broken at Jericho by a man from the tribe of Judah named Achan. As a result, *"...the Lord's anger burned against Israel"* (Joshua 7:1).

Joshua was heartbroken and fell before the

Lord in deep repentance. Then after a re-consecration service, the army marched against Ai once more and the city was totally defeated (Joshua 7:13-8:29).

This was quickly followed by many victories throughout the land.

THE LESSON OF A LIFETIME

After challenges and celebrations, Joshua's farewell address to his followers included these words: *"Be very strong; be careful to obey all that is written in the Book of the Law...without turning aside to the right or to the left"* (Joshua 23:6). And he added, *"One of you routs a thousand, because the Lord your God fights for you, just as he promised. So be very careful to love the Lord your God"* (vv.10-11).

Joshua was a powerful leader because he honored and obeyed a powerful God.

SEIZE YOUR OPPORTUNITY

The media ministry God has allowed us to birth is no accident. It is the direct result of the vision the Lord has placed within me to take the message of Christ outside the walls of our church.

The reason we are touching lives in distant nations of the world is because we seize every opportunity to put the "Go" in the "Gospel."

Members of our congregation may have wondered about the dreams God has unveiled, but I firmly believe the words of the prophet Isaiah: *"I foretold the former things long ago, my mouth announced them and I made them known; then suddenly I acted, and they came to pass"* (Isaiah 48:3).

A Final Chance

I have often pondered what the world would have been like if Noah had told the Lord, "I'm too busy to build the ark."

You see, civilization had been reduced to just one righteous man.

––––––––– ✶ –––––––––

Noah was the only person left whom God trusted.

Starting with the fall of Adam in the Garden, the iniquity of those He created had grown increasingly worse. After several generations, *"The Lord saw how great man's wickedness on the earth had become, and that every inclination of the thoughts of his heart was only evil all the time"* (Genesis 6:5).

Scripture records, *"The Lord was grieved that he had made man on the earth, and his heart was filled with pain. So the Lord said, 'I will wipe* mankind, *whom I have created, from the face of the earth—men and animals, and creatures that move along the ground, and birds of the air—for I am grieved that I have made them* '" (vv.6-7).

In essence, the Almighty was ready to wipe the slate clean and start over.

Righteous and Blameless

Then, as the eyes of the Lord searched across the corners of the earth, He saw one man who was worth sparing. His name was Noah—the grandson of Methuselah, the oldest man who ever lived.

The Bible describes Noah as *"...a righteous man, blameless among the people of his time, and he walked with God"* (v.9).

So the Almighty told Noah what He was about to inflict on this corrupt, violent planet. He declared, *"I am going to put an end to all people, for the earth is filled with violence because of them. I am surely going to destroy both them and the earth"* (v.13).

Then God said, "I want you to build an ark of safety."

THE PLAN

Even more, God described in detail every facet of how the vessel was to be constructed—it's length, width, height, and the kind of wood.

Why an ark? Because God was about to flood the earth with torrential rains which would destroy every living creature. Then the Lord said, *"But I will establish my covenant with you, and you will enter the ark—you and your sons and your wife and your sons' wives with you"* (v.18).

God also instructed Noah to take two of every living creature into the ark with him—and to store enough food to keep them alive until the waters subsided.

"WHAT'S THAT?"

Can you imagine the laughter and ridicule of the neighbors when 500-year-old Noah and his three sons, Shem, Ham and Japheth began assembling planks of cypress wood on the cracked, parched floor of the desert?

"What in the world are you doing?" they asked, bewildered.

"It's going to rain! And I'm building an ark?"

"Rain?" they exclaimed. "What's that? We have never seen rain around here!"

———— ♟ ————

Their comments didn't faze Noah's faith one bit. God had given him this one last opportunity and he wasn't about to let it pass by. He started working.

A 120-YEAR PROJECT

Noah wasn't given the blueprint for a small canoe! The ark was as long as one and a half football fields and as tall as a four story building. Amazing but true, the structure was exactly six times as long as it was wide—and that ratio is the same used by shipbuilders today.

39

God even told him to coat the vessel with "pitch" inside and out (v.14). This tar-like substance made the ark waterproof.

Did the people have time to repent before the flood came? I think so—since Noah worked on the ark for 120 years! They laughed while he toiled, day after day, month after month, year after year and decade after decade until the vessel was completed.

All the time he was calling the people to repentance, yet no one paid any attention to the old man. They thought he had lost his marbles!

"Let Me In!"

Noah made a total commitment to the project because when God gives you a vision, He also supplies you with the energy to complete the task.

Then the Lord told Noah to gather his family and enter the ark—taking with him a male and female of every animal and bird, because, *"Seven days from now I will send rain on the earth for forty days and forty nights, and I will wipe from the face of the earth every living creature I have made"* (Genesis 7:4).

Noah's days of labor were over and he faithfully followed the Lord's command.

Sure enough, in one week a cloud appeared on the horizon—then two, and more. The heavens opened and, just as God promised, it began to rain.

Before long the waters were rising and people were frantically beating on the sides of the ark, screaming, "Let me in! Let me in!" But it was too late.

"BY FAITH"

Since there was no steering or rudder on the vessel, God was the Captain and in total control. The Lord even used His power to shut the door of the ark (v.16).

For the next 40 days and nights the floodwaters

covered the earth—and only Noah, his family and the creatures on board were saved.

The writer of Hebrews says, *"By faith Noah, when warned about things not yet seen, in holy fear built an ark to save his family. By his faith he condemned the world and became heir of the righteousness that comes by faith"* (Hebrew 11:7).

Night is Coming

What is the task God has called you to do? Certainly you have a responsibility to care for your family, but the Lord has a mission He desires you to complete for Him. Remember, *"You will be judged according to your conduct and your actions, declares the Sovereign Lord"* (Ezekiel 24:14).

Jesus was the son of an earthly carpenter, and knew what physical labor was all about, yet He also describes the spiritual dimension: *"As long as it is day, we must do the work of him who sent me. Night is coming, when no one can work"* (John 9:4).

AS IN THE DAYS OF NOAH

The "Night" the Lord is speaking of concerns these end times. He reminds us, *"No one knows about that day or hour, not even the angels in heaven, nor the Son, but only the Father. As it was in the days of Noah, so it will be at the coming of the Son of Man. For in the days before the flood, people were eating and drinking, marrying and giving in marriage, up to the day Noah entered the ark; and they knew nothing about what would happen until the flood came and took them all away. That is how it will be at the coming of the Son of Man"* (Matthew 24:36-39).

God has given you both the strength and the opportunity to work in His harvest. Will you seize the day?

JOIN THE OPTIMIST'S CLUB

A six-year old boy was in his backyard playing baseball all alone. He said to himself, "I'm the greatest batter in the whole world."

Then he threw the ball up in the air, took a swing—and he missed! That was strike one.

He repeated his words, "I'm the greatest batter in the world!" Once more he threw the ball up and took a swing and missed. Strike two!

The same thing happened with the third try. Strike three!

Not willing to be defeated, he thought for a minute, then shouted, "Wow! I'm the greatest PITCHER in the whole world!"

From Good to Great

From grade school to adulthood, we hear much concerning IQ—your Intelligence Quotient. But on a scale of 1 (low) to 100 (high), where would you rank your CQ—Confidence Quotient, or your OQ—Optimism Quotient?

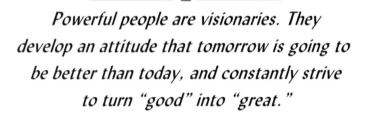

Powerful people are visionaries. They develop an attitude that tomorrow is going to be better than today, and constantly strive to turn "good" into "great."

Jesus tells us, *"Ask and it will be given to you; seek and you will find; knock and the door will be opened to you"* (Matthew 7:7).

However, if you ask for the improper thing, seek what is negative and knock on the wrong door, you'll have tragic results. It is only when you ask in faith *believing* for God's best will you reap a bountiful harvest.

TRUST HIS WORD

You may read the Scriptures every day, but do you trust what the Bible says? Do you have confidence in God when He declares, *"...I will hasten my word to perform it"?* (Jeremiah 1:12 KJV).

———— ♦ ————

God may answer your prayer
today or tomorrow; His calendar is
the only one that counts.

Remember, the Israelites made bricks while in the bondage of Egypt for hundreds of years, yet the Lord did not forget their plight and brought them out.

WHOSE WORD?

Where you commit your trust can have eternal

consequences. Adam and Eve made the tragic mistake of placing their confidence in the word of the serpent over the Word of God.

They had been walking in the realm of the Creator, yet suddenly, by listening to the devil, they entered the physical realm of the enemy. As a result, they ignored the only commandment the Almighty had given them.

In a beautiful paradise, abounding with every good thing, God said, *"You are free to eat from any tree in the garden; but you must not eat from the tree of the knowledge of good and evil, for when you eat of it you will surely die"* (Genesis 2:16-17).

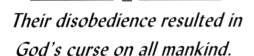

Their disobedience resulted in God's curse on all mankind.

To the woman, He declared, *"I will greatly increase your pains in childbearing"*(Genesis 3:16) and to Adam the Lord said, *"Cursed is the ground because of you; through painful toil you will eat of it all the days of your life"* (v.17).

YOUR RIGHT TO THE TREE

Yes, God has a plan for man's redemption, but if we continue to listen to the word of Satan our trials and troubles will *never* cease.

Because of what happened in the garden we lost the right to the tree of life, yet when we place our confidence in Jesus it is gloriously restored. Thank God, by obeying the Almighty and accepting His Son, we have eternal access to all of the Lord's abundance.

The Bible declares, *"Blessed are they that do his commandments, that they may have right to the tree of life, and may enter in through the gates into the city"* (Revelation 22:14 KJV).

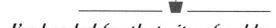

I'm headed for that city of gold and Jesus is my passport. He is seated at the right hand of the Father, ready to welcome me.

Raised to a New Level

If you realize who you are and what God called you to be, your confidence will soar. The psalmist asks this question: *"... what is man that you are mindful of him, the son of man* [mankind] *that you care for him? You made him a little lower than the heavenly beings and crowned him with glory and honor"* (Psalm 8:4-5).

This describes *fallen* man—lower than angels. Yet there is hope. Because of redemption we have been raised to a new level in Christ. Now, all things are under our feet (v.6)—and this includes the angels.

No Apologies Needed

Just before the crucifixion, Pilate asked Jesus the source of His power and authority. He asked the question bluntly: *"Are you the king of the Jews?"* (John 18:33).

Jesus made no apology concerning who He was or what He was to do.

He replied, *"My kingdom is not of this world. If it were, my servants would fight to prevent my arrest by the Jews. But now my kingdom is from another place"* (v.36).

"You are a king, then?" probed Pilate.

Jesus answered, *"You are right in saying I am a king. In fact, for this reason I was born, and for this I came into the world, to testify to the truth. Everyone on the side of truth listens to me"* (v.37).

As followers of Christ we must be confident in who we are—sons and daughters of the Most High. We *"...are the children of God: and if children, then heirs; heirs of God, and joint-heirs with Christ; if so be that we suffer with him, that we may be also glorified together"* (Romans 4:16-17).

What a royal heritage!

A Sneak Preview

I've been asked, "Pastor, when you turn on the news and see terrorist bombings, riots and murder in the streets, aren't you fearful of the future?"

Absolutely not. Why? Because I believe God is in charge of all things, and I've been given a sneak preview of what lies ahead:

- Instead of weeping over man's inhumanity, I see a land where, *"There will be no more death or mourning or crying or pain"* (Revelation 21 4).
- Instead of a polluted world, I see *"...the river of the water of life, as clear as crystal, flowing from the throne of God and of the Lamb"* (Revelation 22:1).
- Instead of the darkness of sin, I see a time when *"There will be no more night...for the Lord God will give them light"* (v.5).

SEEING THE UNSEEN

Don't listen to the defeatists, the naysayers and prophets of doom. A new day is dawning: *"Therefore we do not lose heart. Though outwardly we are wasting away, yet inwardly we are being renewed day by day. For our light and momentary troubles are achieving for us an eternal glory that far outweighs them all. So we fix our eyes not on what is seen, but on what is unseen. For what is seen is temporary, but what is unseen is eternal"* (2 Corinthians 4:16-18).

———— ♥ ————

The same Christ who cleansed your heart from sin, wants to replace your doubts with hope and exchange your fears with faith.

Be *"...confident of this, that he who began a good work in you will carry it on to completion until the day of Christ Jesus"* (Philippians 1:6).

I'm a card-carrying optimist—and I am asking you to join the club!

LISTEN FIRST,
SPEAK LAST

More than once I've seen an upset person walk into a committee meeting and start unloading their anger like a rapid-fire, machine gun.

Finally, when their ammunition was spent and their words exhausted, it was time for others to chime in with their opinions on the matter.

Invariably, there will be one person at the table who doesn't say a word—he or she just sits there observing and listening. But before a decision is made, a committee member will turn to that individual and ask, "Well, what do you think?"

Whether the strategy is planned or not, the

one who speaks last is often the most persuasive voice on the issue. Why? Because there is an awesome power in silence.

It speaks of thoughtfulness, reflection, wisdom and understanding.

THE FEAST AT JERUSALEM

Jesus demonstrated this principle when dealing with His critics.

Once, while in Galilee, He hesitated traveling to Judea since the Jews who lived there were looking for a chance to take His life.

It was time for the Feast of Tabernacles and Jesus' own brothers said to him, *"You ought to leave here and go to Judea, so that your disciples may see the miracles you do. No one who wants to become a public figure acts in secret. Since you are doing these things, show yourself to the world"* (John 7:3-4).

Instead, Jesus told His brothers to go ahead and enjoy the Feast, explaining the time wasn't right for Him to go: *"The world cannot hate you, but it hates me because I testify that what it does is evil"* (v.7).

However, when His family left to attend the Feast, He also journeyed to Jerusalem, staying out of the way and being careful not to draw attention to Himself.

GREAT CONSTERNATION

At the event, the Jews were watching for Jesus, asking, *"Where is that man?"* (v.11). And in the crowd, people whispered about Him. *"Some said, 'He is a good man.' Others replied, 'No, he deceives the people'"* (v.12).

———————— ♦ ————————

The Feast of Tabernacles was half over before Jesus felt He must teach in the temple —and this caused great consternation among the chief priests and Pharisees.

Writing on the Ground

Early the next morning He returned to the temple courts and a large number of people gathered around Him.

Before He uttered a word, the teachers of the law and the Pharisees brought in a woman caught in adultery and made her stand before the group. Then, planing to lay a trap, they said to Jesus, *'Teacher, this woman was caught in the act of adultery. In the Law Moses commanded us to stone such women. Now what do you say?'"* (vv.4-5).

They were hoping His answer would give them a basis to accuse Him.

–––––––––– ⚱ ––––––––––

Jesus didn't give a hasty reply.
Instead He simply listened.

Then, He *"...bent down and started to write on the ground with his finger"* (v.6).

This was more than a simple pause. It gave Him

time to consider His words carefully.

THE SILENT TREATMENT

It was only after they continued questioning Jesus that He straightened up and answered the Pharisees, *"If any one of you is without sin, let him be the first to throw a stone at her"* (v.7).

———— ♦ ————

What did Jesus do next? He gave His critics more of the silent treatment.

The Bible says, *"Again he stooped down and wrote on the ground"* (v.8).

In the quietness of the moment, having been given food for thought, one by one the people began to leave—the older ones first—until only Jesus and the woman remained. He asked her, *"Woman, where are they? Has no one condemned you?"* (v.10).

"No one, sir," she replied.

Jesus declared, *"Then neither do I condemn*

59

Go now and leave your life of sin" (v.11).

LISTENER'S LEARN

The person who talks more than listens may have an audience, but not for long. Soon, their words ring hollow because there is no input, no knowledge or facts to bolster their personal opinions and arguments.

This is why James writes to his fellow believers, *"My dear brothers, take note of this: Everyone should be quick to listen, slow to speak..."* (James 1:19).

King Solomon preached the same principle: *"...let the wise listen and add to their learning, and let the discerning get guidance"* (Proverbs 1:5).

This counsel is especially important concerning your behavior as part of the body of Christ. Scripture tells us, *"Guard your steps when you go to the house of God. Go near to listen rather than to offer the sacrifice of fools, who do not know that they do wrong. Do not be quick with your mouth, do not be hasty in your heart to utter anything before God. God is in heaven and you are on earth, so let your words be few"*(Ecclesiastes 5:1-2).

"BY HEARING"

Prayerfully determine to yourself and to the Lord that you will tame your unruly tongue. *"A fool's mouth is his undoing, and his lips are a snare to his soul"*(Proverbs 18:7).

Remember, hope and expectation are not the result of constant talk. Just the opposite: *"...faith cometh by hearing, and hearing by the word of God"* (Romans 10:17 KJV).

Are you listening?

DON'T BE AFRAID TO MAKE DECISIONS

I was born into a family with a strong spiritual heritage which extends back over 200 years. And since my father and grandfather were preachers, everyone expected me to follow in their footsteps. That was considered a no-brainer!

My parents were shocked when I told them, "I've decided to go to college and study civil engineering."

"Why?" they wanted to know. "That seems so disconnected from the ministry our family has always been involved with."

I tried to explain how if I worked for an architectural engineering firm, it would provide enough money to help finance the work of the Lord. To be honest, in reality I had seen my father and grandfather struggle to build churches and personally, I didn't want to go through such hardship.

No, I didn't separate myself totally from God's Kingdom. In fact, I worked on the blueprints and gave of my physical labor to help my father, Bishop Harry A. Mushegan, build the church on Atlanta's Defoor Avenue.

"God's Rhythm Section"

Dad wouldn't let up!

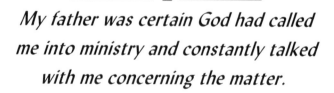

My father was certain God had called me into ministry and constantly talked with me concerning the matter.

Since I loved music, I became involved in the church—enough to satisfy my father and play the songs I enjoyed. We started a youth program with a band called "God's Rhythm Section" which attracted scores of teens to the church and became well known in Georgia and beyond.

In the early 1980s, the call of God on my life was becoming stronger than my will to resist. I had to make a decision. Would it be engineering or evangelism? Drafting or declaring the Word? A secular career or being a full time servant of Christ.

After untold hours of prayer, fasting and seeking the face of God, I made the choice of a lifetime.

———————— ♦ ————————

You can imagine the thrill in the hearts of my godly parents when I told them, "I've decided to spend my future in full time ministry."

In 1982, I became the senior pastor of Gospel Harvester Church.

The Options are Yours

When you study God's Word, you realize the Lord has placed within you an exceptional ability—the power to choose.

He never forces His will or desire on your life. Instead God presents the options and allows you to make the ultimate decision. This includes the small choices we make every day and the crucial ones which determine where we will spend eternity.

Yes, *"God so loved the world that He gave His only begotten Son"*—but read the rest of the verse: *"...that whosoever believeth in him should not perish, but have everlasting life"* (John 3:16 KJV).

The pivotal word is *"believeth."*

Salvation is not automatically given to every person born into this world. We must choose to accept or reject God's plan of redemption.

Scripture makes the outcome clear: *"Whoever believes in the Son has eternal life, but whoever rejects the Son will not see life, for God's wrath remains on him"* (John 3:36).

LIFE OR DEATH?

Thousands of years ago, the Almighty made a divine offer.

―――――――― ♦ ――――――――

God instructed Moses to tell the people that if they obeyed the Lord and kept His covenants, every promise from heaven would be theirs.

Then, to make it personal, God said through His servant, *"Now what I am commanding you today is not too difficult for you or beyond your reach. It is not up in heaven, so that you have to ask, 'Who will ascend into heaven to get it and*

67

proclaim it to us so we may obey it?' Nor is it beyond the sea, so that you have to ask, 'Who will cross the sea to get it and proclaim it to us so we may obey it?' No, the word is very near you; it is in your mouth and in your heart so you may obey it" (Deuteronomy 30:11-14).

Then God presented the choices: " *See, I set before you today life and prosperity, death and destruction"* (v.15).

If you *"walk in his ways"* (v.16) there will be increase, but if your *"heart turns away* [and] *you are not obedient"* (v.17), "you will certainly be destroyed" (v.18).

And here's the bottom line: *"This day I call heaven and earth as witnesses against you that I have set before you life and death, blessings and curses. Now choose life, so that you and your children may live"* (v. 19).

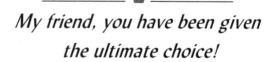

My friend, you have been given the ultimate choice!

THE KING'S DECREE

I always enjoy reading the story of Daniel. Here was a Jewish boy who was brought into the palace of King Nebuchadnezzar when the Babylonians conquered Jerusalem. His leadership abilities were so outstanding that he served three royal families.

Finally, under King Darius, *"Daniel so distinguished himself among the administrators and the satraps by his exceptional qualities that the king planned to set him over the whole kingdom"* (Daniel 6:3).

As you can imagine, this didn't sit too well with the other governors, so they conspired to oust him.

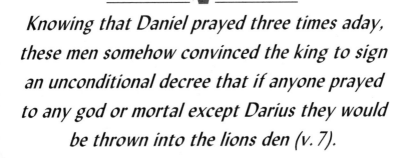

Knowing that Daniel prayed three times a day, these men somehow convinced the king to sign an unconditional decree that if anyone prayed to any god or mortal except Darius they would be thrown into the lions den (v. 7).

PRAYING IN THE WINDOW

When Daniel learned of the new law, he made the most important decision of his life. He would continue to pray to the Living God of heaven in his house as he always had—at an upstairs window that opened toward Jerusalem.

Of course, the conspirators saw Daniel praying and quickly ran to Dairus. But the law was the law—even though the king tried every way possible to extricate Daniel out of the predicament in which he had been placed.

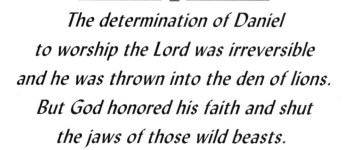

The determination of Daniel
to worship the Lord was irreversible
and he was thrown into the den of lions.
But God honored his faith and shut
the jaws of those wild beasts.

This resulted in a new mandate by the king.

Standing before the people he announceed: *"I issue a decree that in every part of my kingdom people must fear and reverence the God of Daniel. For he is the living God and he endures forever; his kingdom will not be destroyed, his dominion will never end He rescues and he saves; he performs signs and wonders in the heavens and on the earth. He has rescued Daniel from the power of the lions"* (vv.26-27).

Daniel's decision brought revival across the land.

FIRST THINGS FIRST

Our choices must never be based on logic and intellect alone.

———————— ⚘ ————————

Yes, God gives us reasoning power which we are to use, but the only way to discern the Father's will is to spend time with Him in prayer.

Jesus was the Son of God, yet before every major decision while He walked this earth, He prayed to His Father in heaven. For example, when it was time to chose the twelve disciples who would accompany Him in ministry, the Bible says, *"Jesus went out to a mountainside to pray, and spent the night praying to God. When morning came, he called his disciples to him and chose twelve of them, whom he also designated apostles"* (Luke 6:12-13).

———————— ♦ ————————

Today, and every day of your life, commune and fellowship with the Lord and make sure your goals and objectives mirror His will.

As King Solomon says, *"In his heart a man plans his course, but the Lord determines his steps"* (Proverbs 16:9).

Our Heavenly Father is still asking this vital question: *"...choose for yourselves this day whom you will serve"* (Joshua 24:15).

I pray you will stand tall and tell the world: "As for me and my house, we will serve the Lord!"

NEVER SETTLE FOR SECOND BEST

Going first class isn't about buying the most expensive plane ticket or going into debt for a luxury automobile. No, it's an *attitude*, a mind-set and a decision concerning how you will live your life.

As a minister, I've visited the homes of humble families who could barely make ends meet, yet their houses were spotless, their children neatly dressed and you could sense their commitment to quality living.

On the other hand, I have been around some individuals whose bank accounts are staggering, yet their homes look like a tornado just blew through and they forgot to clean up the debris! I wonder, "How can these people have so much money and take no pride in how they live or dress?"

YOUR ROYAL FAMILY

Personally, I believe every blood-bought, born again believer should take a serious look at their lifestyle. Since we are representatives of the King of kings, and Lord of lords, shouldn't we act accordingly?

- Your Father owns *"...the cattle on a thousand hills"* (Psalm 50:10).
- The Almighty declares, *"The silver is mine and the gold is mine "* (Haggai 2:8).
- And *"...God will meet all your needs according to his glorious riches in Christ Jesus"* (Philippians 4:19).

Since your eternal life begins the moment you accept Christ as your personal Savior, this means your inheritance begins right now!

Some believers think you have to wait until you get to heaven to receive God's promises. No. An inheritance begins when an individual dies—and Jesus died once and for all at Calvary.

This means what belongs to the Father, belongs to the Son, and *"...if we are children, then we are heirs—heirs of God and co-heirs with Christ"* (Romans 8:17).

———— ♦ ————

As a member of a royal family,
your speech, your conduct and how you
live must be worthy of your Father.

This is why you should, *"Do your best to present yourself to God as one approved, a workman who does not need to be ashamed..."* (2 Timothy 2:15).

AN UNEXPECTED BONUS

By any measure or comparison, King Solomon

is still the richest man who ever lived. But we often forget why he was given such great wealth.

Remember, this was the son of a one-time shepherd boy named David. And when Solomon replaced him as King, he was a humble servant of the Lord.

At a place called Gibeon, where he went to offer sacrifices, God appeared to him, saying, *"Ask for whatever you want me to give you"* (1 Kings 3:5).

Solomon looked up to the Lord and confessed, *"...I am only a little child and do not know how to carry out my duties...So give your servant a discerning heart to govern your people and to distinguish between right and wrong. For who is able to govern this great people of yours?"* (vv.7,9).

God gave Solomon this reply: *"Since you have asked for this and not for long life or wealth for yourself, nor have asked for the death of your enemies but for discernment in administering justice, I will do what you have asked. I will give you a wise and discerning heart, so that there will never have been anyone like you, nor will there ever be"* (vv.11-12).

Then the Lord added a bonus Solomon certainly wasn't expecting: *"Moreover, I will give you what you have not asked for—both riches and honor—so that in your lifetime you will have no equal among kings"* (v.13).

A MAGNIFICENT PROJECT

From that day forward, the blessings and bounty of heaven began to rain down on Solomon. His kingdom was expanded and "tribute" was brought to him from every corner of the land (1 Kings 4:21). To give you just a glimpse of his power and wealth, he had, *"...four thousand stalls for chariot horses, and twelve thousand horses"* (v.26).

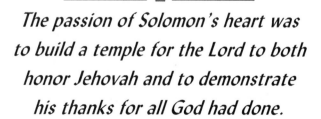

The passion of Solomon's heart was to build a temple for the Lord to both honor Jehovah and to demonstrate his thanks for all God had done.

This was no Home Depot building project!

With plans for the most magnificent structure ever built, he assembled:

- 30,000 men to bring cedar and pine from Lebanon (1 Kings 5:13).
- 70,000 carriers 80,000 stone cutters (v.15).
- 3,300 foremen to supervise the workmen (v.16).
- Expert craftsmen and artisans from the region (v.18).

OH, WHAT SPLENDOR

What a glorious edifice! The inner sanctuary, where the Ark of the Covenant was placed was *"overlaid...with pure gold"* (1 Kings 6: 20). There were ornate carvings of cherubim, palm trees and flowers (v.29).

It took thirteen years to complete the project—and you will understand why if you read the two chapters of the Bible which describe the amazing details of the temple (I Kings 6,7). The words "excellence" and "quality" are an understatement.

HE'S SAVING THE BEST

What the Lord blesses us with is far above "average," and we need to be willing to present the same to Him.

_____ ♦ _____

The very first miracle Jesus ever performed on earth tells us there is no comparison to what He offers.

At the wedding in Cana, when the guests ran out of wine, Jesus asked for two large containers of water to be filled to the brim. Then He told the attendants, *"Now draw some out and take it to the master of the banquet"* (John 2:8).

When the man tasted the water which had been turned into wine (not knowing it was a miracle of God), he turned to the bridegroom and commented, *"Everyone brings out the choice wine first and then the cheaper wine after the guests have had too much to drink; but you have saved the best till now"*(v.10).

We serve a Lord who exceeds above and beyond all we ask or think (Ephesians 3:20).

THE QUALITIES GOD EXPECTS

Friend, let me encourage you to make excellence your passion. A good place to begin is to adopt the character values and qualities recommended by Peter. He counsels: *"...make every effort to add to your faith goodness; and to goodness, knowledge; and to knowledge, self-control; and to self-control, perseverance; and to perseverance, godliness; and to godliness, brotherly kindness; and to brotherly kindness, love. For if you possess these qualities in increasing measure, they will keep you from being ineffective and unproductive in your knowledge of our Lord Jesus Christ"* (2 Peter 1:5-8).

The apostle Paul adds to this list by telling us,

"...whatever is true, whatever is noble, whatever is right, whatever is pure, whatever is lovely, whatever is admirable—if anything is excellent or praiseworthy—think about such things" (Philippians 4:8).

One day soon, we will stand before God and present an account of ourselves to Him (Romans 14:12). Your life *"will be shown for what it is...[and] revealed with fire, and the fire will test the quality of each man's work"* (1 Corinthians 3:13).

Will you pass the "excellence" test?

SWALLOW YOUR PRIDE

The noted British preacher, Dr. G. Campbell Morgan, had four sons—all of whom became outstanding ministers in their own right.

At a family reunion, a friend asked one of the sons, "Which Morgan is the greatest preacher?"

While the son looked at his father, he quickly replied, "My mother!"

A DECISION OF THE HEART

Deflecting praise and walking the road of humility is a powerful virtue. However, it is not one which can be acquired by practice or learned in an acting class. Genuine meekness springs from a decision of the heart—and is expressed by your true nature and personality.

TOTAL TRUST

Scripture presents sterling examples of men and women with humble spirits.

For example, Job was a man of great wealth, yet God trusted him without question. So much so that when Satan was looking for someone to tempt, the Lord said, *"Have you considered my servant Job? There is no one on earth like him; he is blameless and upright, a man who fears God and shuns evil"* (Job 1:8). In other words, the Lord didn't punish Job, rather He *allowed* him to endure a time of great testing.

The devil began his torment, afflicting Job *"...with painful sores from the soles of his feet to the top of his head. Then Job took a piece of broken pottery and scraped himself with it as he sat among the ashes"* (Job 2:7-8).

However, in the midst of this terrible ordeal,

Job didn't lose his faith. At one point, He declared, *"Though he slay me, yet will I trust in him"* (Job 13:15 KJV).

A DOUBLE PORTION

Again and again, Job expressed his real humility to the Lord. He looked up to heaven and said, *"I know that you can do all things; no plan of yours can be thwarted. You asked, 'Who is this that obscures my counsel without knowledge?' Surely I spoke of things I did not understand, things too wonderful for me to know. You said, 'Listen now, and I will speak; I will question you, and you shall answer me.' My ears had heard of you but now my eyes have seen you. Therefore I despise myself and repent in dust and ashes"* (Job 42:2-6).

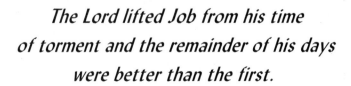

The Lord lifted Job from his time of torment and the remainder of his days were better than the first.

God not only restored his wealth—He gave him a double portion (Job 42:12).

AN UNUSUAL REQUEST

During the three years of Jesus' ministry on earth, He used many opportunities to establish the importance of a humble walk.

On the road to Jerusalem, where Jesus was about to be handed over to the officials, He took the twelve disciples aside and told them what to expect in the days ahead. He said, *"...the Son of Man will be betrayed to the chief priests and the teachers of the law. They will condemn him to death and will turn him over to the Gentiles to be mocked and flogged and crucified. On the third day he will be raised to life!"* (Matthew 20:18-19).

About this same time, the mother of James and John knelt before Jesus—along with her two sons.

"What is it you want?" Jesus asked her.

She said, *"Grant that one of these two sons of mine may sit at your right and the other at your left in your kingdom"* (v.21)

Jesus answered, "You don't know what you're asking." Then He turned to James and John and asked, *"Can you drink the cup I am going to drink?"* (v.22).

They assured Him they could.

Jesus explained they would certainly drink from His cup, *"...but to sit at my right or left is not for me to grant. These places belong to those for whom they have been prepared by my Father"* (v.23).

HE CAME TO SERVE

When the ten other disciples heard of this conversation they were quite upset with the two brothers. Jesus calmed them down by explaining how godless rulers abuse their power, "but it is not going to be that way with you."

Instead, He said, *"whoever wants to become great among you must be your servant, and whoever wants to be first must be your slave—just as the Son of Man did not come to be served, but to serve, and to give his life as a ransom for many"* (vv.26-28).

It was a challenging lesson in humility.

THE SECRET OF BEING EXALTED

Jesus had great respect for the law of Moses which was taught in the temple, yet He did not think too highly of the Pharisees, who *"do not practice what they preach"* (Matthew 23:3).

As an example, Jesus said, *"They tie up heavy loads and put them on men's shoulders, but they themselves are not willing to lift a finger to move them"* (v.4).

He explained how everything these men did was for show—always seeking the place of honor at banquets and claiming the most prestigious seats in the synagogues.

Furthermore, He told His disciples, *"...they*

love to be greeted in the marketplaces and to have men call them 'Rabbi.' But you are not to be called 'Rabbi,' for you have only one Master and you are all brothers. And do not call anyone on earth 'father,' for you have one Father, and he is in heaven. Nor are you to be called 'teacher,' for you have one Teacher, the Christ" (vv.7-10).

Then He declared this divine principle: *"The greatest among you will be your servant. For whoever exalts himself will be humbled, and whoever humbles himself will be exalted"* (vv.11-12).

"VAIN CONCEIT?"

The apostle Paul may have been writing to the believers at Philippi, yet his words contain a strong truth for you and me. He says, *"Do nothing out of selfish ambition or vain conceit, but in humility consider others better than yourselves. Each of you should look not only to your own interests, but also to the interests of others"* (Philippians 2:3-4).

Paul says our attitude should be a reflection of

Christ, *"Who, being in very nature God, did not consider equality with God something to be grasped, but made himself nothing, taking the very nature of a servant, being made in human likeness. And being found in appearance as a man, he humbled himself and became obedient to death—death on a cross! Therefore God exalted him to the highest place and gave him the name that is above every name, that at the name of Jesus every knee should bow, in heaven and on earth and under the earth, and every tongue confess that Jesus Christ is Lord, to the glory of God the Father"* (vv.6-11).

If being a Christian means we are to be "Christ-like," we must be serious concerning living the life of a servant.

GRACE FOR THE HUMBLE

Power for power's sake is a short road to

failure. It undermines leadership, destroys relationships and isolates the man or woman who tries to manage, supervise or motivate others using this strategy.

Peter tells us, *"...clothe yourselves with humility toward one another, because, 'God opposes the proud but gives grace to the humble.' Humble yourselves, therefore, under God's mighty hand, that he may lift you up in due time"* (1 Peter 5:5-6).

Perhaps it's time for you to have a talk with the Lord—confessing your weaknesses and asking for His strength. Pray, "Lord, give me a contrite spirit and a humble heart."

Bid a final farewell to false pride!

DEMONSTRATE YOUR FAITH AND BELIEF

If you were asked to name the most powerful people in Old Testament times, surely Abraham would be high on your list.

When you read the chronicle of his life, you'll find the reason for his outstanding place in history.

The Almighty once asked Abraham to *"Look up at the heavens and count the stars—if indeed you can count them"* (Genesis 15:5). Then He said, *"So shall your offspring be."*

In the next verse we find the secret of why Abraham became such an effective leader. The Bible declares, he *"...believed the Lord"* (v.6).

His entire life was one of devout faith and

unwavering belief:

- *"By faith Abraham, when called to go to a place he would later receive as his inheritance, obeyed and went, even though he did not know where he was going"* (Hebrews 11:8).
- *"By faith Abraham, even though he was past age—and Sarah herself was barren—was enabled to become a father because he considered him faithful who had made the promise"* (v.11).
- *"By faith Abraham, when God tested him, offered Isaac as a sacrifice. He who had received the promises was about to sacrifice his one and only son"* (v.17).

HE PRAYED!

Prayer and divine expectation followed

Abraham all his days. If fact, every time he made a major decision, he stopped to build an altar to honor the Lord. He did this at Shechem (Genesis 12:7), Bethel (v.8), Hebron (Genesis 13:18) plus other significant locations where God had blessed him.

Later, when the sin of Sodom and Gomorrah was revealed, Abraham prayed—"standing before the Lord" (Genesis 18:22).

He was believing for deliverance!

HALF-BELIEF?

There is no such thing as *partial* faith or lukewarm confidence in God. You either have it or you don't.

_____ ♦ _____

Some say, "I sort of believe," or
"I almost have faith."

Would you be as casual concerning a bridge you are about to drive over, a bank which holds your investments or the electrical wiring system in your home which houses your loved ones?

As a Christian, half-belief is denying God's Word and declaring His promises to be unreliable. In fact, *"...without faith it is impossible to please God, because anyone who comes to him must believe that he exists and that he rewards those who earnestly seek him"* (Hebrews 11:6).

THE "FOURTH MAN"

Shadrach, Meshach and Abednego didn't make it unscathed out of the fiery furnace with part-time faith. It was because of their total reliance on God that the "Fourth Man" appeared to them in the midst of the flames. As a result, they walked out of the inferno without their clothes being singed or the smell of smoke on their bodies.

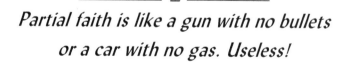

Partial faith is like a gun with no bullets or a car with no gas. Useless!

It is futile to seek after something in which you do not truly believe with all of your heart and soul.

Many individuals pursue their personal desires, but not the Lord's will. However, scripture doesn't tell us, "If you believe in yourself, the sky's the limit." No, Jesus says, *"With man this is impossible, but with God all things are possible"* (Matthew 19:26).

ALL OR NOTHING

Faith is one of the most abused words in Scripture—due to a lack of our understanding. It is not a gift we do *not* have, rather something we possess, yet have not accessed. According to Scripture, *"...God hath dealt to every man* [a] *measure of faith"* (Romans 12:3 KJV).

Many have faith for their own salvation, yet refuse to believe for the abundant life, healing, divine guidance, protection the bounty of heaven.

But how can faith be separated? You either have faith for all, or for none.

Even *"...if you have faith as small as a mustard seed, you can say to this mountain, 'Move from here to there' and it will move. Nothing will be impossible for you"* (Matthew 17:20).

The end of the matter is whatever God says.

HAVE YOU HEARD?

If what we pray for does not come to pass immediately, we tell ourselves we have a lack of faith. This is a copout. How can a man lack what he does not understand?

This is illustrated in Scripture when Paul came to Ephesus and, during a conversation with twelve believers, he asked, *"Did you receive the Holy Spirit when you believed?"* (Acts 19:2).

They answered, *"No, we have not even heard that there is a Holy Spirit"* (v.2).

These people were without knowledge. So Paul questioned them further: *"Then what baptism did you receive?"* (v.3).

"John's baptism," they replied.

Paul explained, *"John's baptism was a baptism of repentance. He told the people to believe in the one coming after him, that is, in Jesus. On hearing this, they were baptized into the name of the Lord Jesus"* (vv. 4-5).

Immediately, Paul laid his hands on the twelve and they received the same Holy Spirit which was outpoured on the believers in the Upper Room.

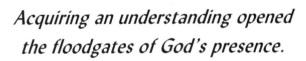

Acquiring an understanding opened the floodgates of God's presence.

This is why we must give priority to the study of the Word regarding this matter.

FAITH THAT WALKS!

Wherever Jesus went, crowds gathered, and in a village near Galilee, a ruler of the local synagogue named Jairus, knelt before Him and pleaded, *"My little daughter is dying. Please come and put your hands on her so that she will be healed and live"* (Mark 5:23).

The Bible doesn't tell us whether or not this man was a follower of Christ. He probably wasn't since the religious leaders of the day were highly critical of Jesus. But when your daughter is dying, being politically correct falls by the wayside. You don't care what your friends and colleagues think.

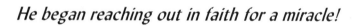

He began reaching out in faith for a miracle!

Jesus, filled with compassion, granted the man's request and—along with His disciples—began walking towards the distraught father's home.

One the way, a few people rushed from the leader's house and informed him, *"Your daughter is dead...Why bother the teacher any more?"* (v.35).

"Get Out!"

Jesus heard those words and told the synagogue ruler, *"Don't be afraid; just believe"* (v.36).

When they reached the house, the Lord asked the pressing crowd to stay back. Only the father, Peter, James and John walked inside with Jesus.

Assembled in the home were a large group of neighbors, howling in grief, playing musical instruments and making a great deal of noise. Jesus silenced the mourners and said, *"Why all this commotion and wailing? The child is not dead but asleep"* (v. 39).

They began laughing and ridiculing such a suggestion. Immediately, He ordered all of them out of the house.

Every time I read this story, I think of the congregations today who like to play their loud music and shout, yet the ministry is hollow and lifeless. If they would only listen, they would hear the Lord saying, "Leave this place! I want to raise up a glorious church."

"Get Up!"

In the home of the Jewish ruler, Jesus wasn't about to perform any mighty works in the presence of doubters. *"After he put them all out, he took the child's father and mother and the disciples who were with him, and went in where the child was. He took her by the hand and said to her, 'Talitha koum!' (which means, 'Little girl, I say to you, get up!')"* (vv.40-41).

Instantly this twelve-year-old girl stood to her feet and walked around. She was healed!

A Matter of Sight

Faith has eyes—and without it you are sightless. Remember, when two blind men came to Jesus, He touched their eyes and said, *"According to your faith will it be done to you"* (Matthew 9:29). And their sight was restored.

On the road to Damascus, when Saul (who

became the apostle Paul) was struck by the power of God, Jesus gave him a new mission. He would go and minister to the people, *"...to open their eyes and turn them from darkness to light, and from the power of Satan to God, so that they may receive forgiveness of sins and a place among those who are sanctified by faith in me"* (Acts 26:18).

Spiritual eyes are opened wide by faith.

THE ULTIMATE!

Sadly, there are those who have *little* faith, and some are guilty of *convenient* faith—only using their belief when it's advantageous. However, the Lord desires that we have *ultimate* faith.

When something is referred to as the *ultimate,* it means the best example of its kind. The word itself is derived from the Latin term "ultimas" —for "come to an end."

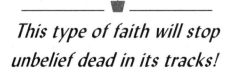

This type of faith will stop unbelief dead in its tracks!

SEEING THE POSSIBILITIES

Ultimate faith will not allow you to see what you do not have, rather it enables you to view the place of provision the Lord has prepared.

When five thousand people gathered on the side of a hill to listen to Jesus teach, the hour arrived when the people needed something to eat. The disciples said to the Lord, *"Send the crowds away, so they can go to the villages and buy themselves some food"* (Matthew 14:15).

Jesus answered, *"They do not need to go away. You give them something to eat"* (v.16).

All they could find was a young boy with his lunch, so the disciples rushed back and told Jesus, *"We have here only five loaves of bread and two fish"* (v.17).

HE SAW A BANQUET!

How typical. They saw and focused on what

they *didn't* have—which wasn't nearly enough. This reminds me of people today who put themselves down and complain, "I didn't come from the right side of the tracks. I don't have a proper education. I'm not financially able to launch my career."

———————— ♦ ————————

However, the Lord didn't see just a few meager loaves of bread and a couple of fish, He saw a banquet for 5,000!

Jesus told the disciples, *"Bring them here to me"* (v.18)—and directed the people to sit down on the grass. Then He blessed the provisions, broke the loaves and gave them to the disciples to distribute to the people.

The Bible records, *"They all ate and were satisfied, and the disciples picked up twelve basketfuls of broken pieces that were left over"* (v.20).

What belief!

"Peace Be Still"

Faith is an internal understanding of who you are in relationship to God's Word.

This being the case, my life is not dependent on luck or chance, but favor. And my favor relies on my faith in the Word of Jehovah.

I pray you will allow the Lord to be involved in every choice you make.

Faith says, "I do not want to make a decision or step out of the boat unless You are there with me. The waves are high and the seas too rough to make it safely to shore by myself."

By making this your declaration, you will hear Him say, *"Peace, be still"* (Mark 4:39 KJV) and you will enter into His perfect rest.

Doing "All Things"

Ultimate faith doesn't answer questions with the word "If." Rather it says, "I'm ready to see this vision come to pass."

Faith speaks to my inability and allows me to accomplish what I could never do alone.

————— ♦ —————

When failures appear, divine belief steps in and allows me to put my mistakes behind me.

A real leader believes, *"I can do all things through Christ which strengtheneth me"* (Philippians 4:13 KJV).

A WARNING

Our season of life on earth is short. This is not a time for playing games with God. Every believer needs to abandon any phony façade and move to a genuine faith.

The Bible says in the last days, *"People will be lovers of themselves, lovers of money, boastful, proud, abusive, disobedient to their parents, ungrateful, unholy, without love, unforgiving, slanderous, without self-control, brutal, not lovers of the good, treacherous, rash, conceited, lovers of pleasure rather than lovers of God—having a form of godliness but denying its power. Have nothing to do with them"* (2 Timothy 3:1-5).

Beware of wolves wearing sheep's clothing!

WHAT'S ON THE BRANCHES?

Is there evidence of faith in your life?

———————— ♆ ————————

Are there buds on your tree getting ready to produce spiritual fruit?

Jesus was walking with His disciples when He saw a fig tree which should have been laden with fruit, but all it had were leaves. As a result, Jesus said. *"May you never bear fruit again!"* (Matthew 21:19).

Immediately the tree withered and died.

When the Lord looks into your life, what does He see? Is there fruit growing on the branches?

Jesus is still walking the streets today, hungry to find those who have a measure of faith. To you He says, *"If you believe, you will receive whatever you ask for in prayer"* (v.22).

By a miracle, He will multiply your "measure" into ultimate faith.

GIVE CREDIT TO YOUR TEAM

The Super Bowl of life has never been won by a single individual—it is always the result of a united effort.

There were two reasons David *"became more and more powerful"* (1 Chronicles 11:9):

1. Because *"...the Lord Almighty was with him"* (v.9)
2. Because of *"...David's mighty men—they, together with all Israel, gave his kingship strong support to extend it over the whole land, as the Lord had promised"* (v.10).

They weren't called "David's mighty men" simply because they were super heroes, but because of the relationship he had with them. That is what made these men such a formidable force.

————————— ♦ —————————

Power multiplies when we are in complete agreement—in unity.

This is how one can chase a thousand and two can put 10,000 to flight (Deuteronomy 32:20).

SUCCESS IS A TEAM EFFORT

The devil works overtime attempting to keep God's people divided, because he knows when we join forces he is on the losing side.

Look at the results of these high-impact teams in Bible times:

Elijah and Elisha

Young Elisha was plowing in a field when the

great prophet, Elijah, *"...went up to him and threw his cloak around him"* (1 Kings 19:19).

Immediately, Elisha left his work and the two began ministering together with the presence of Almighty God. And when it was time for Elijah to be taken up into heaven, Elisha said again and again, *"As surely as the Lord lives and as you live, I will not leave you"* (2 Kings 2:2,4,6).

Because of his devoted faithfulness, when Elijah ascended in a whirlwind, his mantle—and a double portion of his anointing—fell on Elisha.

Esther and Mordecai

Her beauty and personal charm led Esther to become the Queen of Persia. The king, however, did not know she was an orphaned Jewish girl who had been raised by her uncle, Mordecai.

After learning that the prime minister, Haman, had devised a plan to kill every Jew living in the kingdom, Mordecai secretly shared the news with Esther.

Taking her life in her hands and saying, *"...if I*

perish, I perish" (Esther 4:16), she exposed the plot —and Haman was hung on the same gallows he had built for Mordecai

---

It was because of the relationship between Esther and Mordecai the Jewish people were saved.

David and Jonathan

When King Saul grew so jealous of David that he wanted to kill him, Saul's own son, Jonathan, protected David. The Bible says, *"...Jonathan made a covenant with David because he loved him as himself"* (1 Samuel 18:3).

From that moment on, the two looked after each other's interests.

Paul and Barnabus

These two first-century missionaries traveled to Cyprus, Asia Minor and Greece. The Bible records how they risked their lives for the sake of Christ (Acts 15:26).

It was while Paul and Barnabus ministered together for an entire year in Antioch that followers of Jesus were first called "Christians" (Acts 11:26).

Jesus and the Disciples

As the Son of God, Jesus certainly had the power and authority to represent the Father on earth. Why then, did He choose twelve disciples?

Christ knew He would one day ascend back to heaven, and for God's work to continue, He chose these men so the church would be established after His departure.

In addition, this was a pattern for leadership in the fulfilling of the Great Commission.

Not only did Jesus choose the twelve, but He also appointed seventy others and *"...sent them two by two ahead of him to every town and place where he was about to go"* (Luke 10:1).

He did this because the harvest was plentiful, *"...but the workers are few"* (v.2).

They returned with glorious reports, exclaiming, *"Lord, even the demons submit to us in your name"*(v.17).

Two Will Become One

The call to relationship is at the heart of living according to God's principles. It is demonstrated by the biblical view of marriage.

Jesus says, *"For this reason a man will leave his father and mother and be united to his wife, and the two will become one flesh. So they are no longer two, but one. Therefore what God has joined together, let man not separate"* (Matthew 19:5-6).

It's not simply "a good idea" for us to live in harmony, it is the Father's command.

One Plants, Another Waters

The apostle Paul preached a powerful message concerning teamwork to the believers at Corinth. He said, *"I planted the seed, Apollos watered it, but God made it grow. So neither he who plants nor he who waters is anything, but only God, who makes things grow. The man who plants and the man who waters have one purpose, and each will be rewarded according to his own labor. For we are God's fellow workers; you are God's field, God's building"* (1 Corinthians 3:7-10).

———— ♦ ————

Paul fully understood that he was only laying the foundation for others to build upon.

MANY PARTS—ONE BODY

The church—the body of Christ—is meant to be an example of how each of us, can work together for the common good.

As Scripture explains, *"To one there is given through the Spirit the message of wisdom, to another the message of knowledge by means of the same Spirit, to another faith by the same Spirit, to another gifts of healing by that one Spirit, to another miraculous powers, to another prophecy, to another distinguishing between spirits, to* another speaking in different kinds of tongues, and to still another the interpretation of tongues. All these are the work of one and the same Spirit, and he gives them to each one, just as he determines" (1 Corinthians 12:8-11).

What is the benefit of this diversity of gifts in the church? "The body is a unit, though it is made up of many parts; and though all its parts are many, they form one body. So it is with Christ" (v.12).

IN ONE ACCORD

Make certain your relationships are in line with God's vision.

In the days of Amos, the people were out of step with the plans of the Almighty. This is why the Lord questioned, "Do two walk together unless they have agreed to do so?" (Amos 3:3). God was saying, "Why should you expect My blessings if you have refused to obey my commands?"

The Lord will only give revelation to those who

are in accord with Him.

A UNITED HOUSE

We must lay aside our own objectives, plans and desires—and do what the Lord has called us to accomplish. This means finding our place in God's Kingdom and fulfilling His work and His will together.

Jesus tells us, *"Every kingdom divided against itself will be ruined, and every city or household divided against itself will not stand"* (Matthew 12:25).

———————— 🕯 ————————

If we are separated in our thoughts (double minded), we won't be able to survive because we will have a shaky foundation.

Singleness of purpose, in unity with God's plan and with those He has placed in our midst, leads to triumph. We must declare—despite what is happening around us—"I know my purpose in life and I will join myself with like-minded believers to accomplish the task."

As the psalmist writes, *"How good and pleasant it is when brothers live together in unity"* (Psalm 133:1).

Today, start tapping into the power source of teamwork—and don't hesitate to give others the credit.

STAY FOCUSED ON YOUR MISSION

Late in the morning on Thursday, July 4, 1776, church bells began ringing all over Philadelphia. The Continental Congress, meeting at the Pennsylvania State House had just made world history.

In a bold move into uncharted waters, representatives from the thirteen American colonies under England's rule passed the Declaration of Independence. They would no longer pledge their allegiance to the British Crown.

The 56 men who signed this document were placing their lives on the line—and their futures in jeopardy. They knew the penalty would be death if they were captured.

Who were these brave Americans? Among them were 24 lawyers, 14 farmers, 12 merchants, four physicians, one manufacturer and a minister of the Gospel—Rev. John Witherspoon who was the first president of what is now Princeton University.

"Our Sacred Honor"

Let's take a close look at what happened to these courageous patriots:

- Five were captured by the British as traitors and tortured before they died.
- Twelve had their homes ransacked and burned.
- Two lost their sons in the Revolutionary War, another had two sons captured.
- Nine fought and died from wounds or the hardships of the war.
- Seventeen lost everything they owned.

These men were not just casually putting ink on paper; they valued liberty more than what they owned or possessed.

Their very life's blood was spilled for the freedom you and I enjoy today.

Standing tall in the face of tyranny, they made this vow: "For the support of this Declaration with a firm reliance on the protection of divine providence, we mutually pledge to each other our lives, our fortunes and our sacred honor."

A LICENSE TO SIN?

Today, the struggle still rages. Only now the battleground is in the halls of justice and the courts of public opinion. The war is over the definition of marriage, our right to pray in public or to display the Ten Commandments on which the nation was founded.

Those who protest are abusing the rights of a country formed by people who trusted in God. Sad but true, the only reason citizens can openly flaunt their ungodly lifestyle is because of the Declaration for which these men paid the ultimate price. Now our citizens take liberty as a license to sin—adopting "situational" theology to justify carnality.

"ENOUGH IS ENOUGH!"

If you want to practice the principles of powerful people, adopt the faith and integrity of our Founding Fathers.

When we look at the wars which followed their righteous stand, we must ask this question: Did we shed our blood for the nations of the world just to have them mock and laugh at us?

———— ♛ ————

It's time to stand up and say,
"Enough is enough!"

It takes committed people to bring about reformation and change—those who will proclaim, "We will speak out for our God and will not be bound by sin. We have been set free by the power of the Lord and are moving forward."

SALT AND LIGHT

Jesus is still saying to us: *"You are the salt of the earth. But if the salt loses its saltiness, how can it be made salty again? It is no longer good for anything, except to be thrown out and trampled by men"* (Matthew 5:13).

In Bible times salt was a precious commodity which was traded like gold.

Why did God say this? Because in His eyes we are important, not just to the heavenlies but to this earth. The church is the salt which contains healing properties and helps season and preserve believers.

Jesus also declared, *"You are the light of the world"* (v.14). If you question whether light is important, let the sun be dimmed—and I shudder to think what the world would be like without the church. All hell would break loose!

REBUILD THE WALLS

Where are the Nehemiahs of our world? Here was a man who was motivated by purpose and driven by passion.

Nehemiah was in exile when he learned the walls of his beloved city of Jerusalem were broken down and its famed gates had been burned with fire. As he writes, *"When I heard these things, I sat down and wept. For some days I mourned and fasted and prayed before the God of heaven"* (Nehemiah 1:4).

He was also spurred into action, forming a monumental effort to rebuild the walls. In the process, he was joined by like-minded men from throughout the region—Jericho, Gibeon, and beyond

Sanballat, an official of the kingdom who hated

the Israelites, came to mock those who diligently worked on the project. He asked, *"What are those feeble Jews doing?"* (Nehemiah 4:2). And his friend, Tobiah, said, *"What they are building— if even a fox climbed up on it, he would break down their wall of stones!"* (v.3).

Such words only infused Nehemiah and his men to build with more determination than ever. Physical attacks came and they *"....did their work with one hand and held a weapon in the other"* (v.17).

The reason the project was successfully completed is because they caught the passion of the leader and *"...the people had a mind to work"* (v.6 KJV).

INTERNAL DIRECTION

Powerful people not only have goals, they have vision—because without it they would perish (Proverbs 29:18).

———————— ♦ ————————

*It is your spiritual eyes which allow you to see
the direction in which you are headed.*

Have you ever driven down an Interstate
highway in the rain when suddenly a huge truck
passes by? For a few seconds you are blinded by
the spray! You have to depend on your instincts to
survive.

This also happens when you are deluged by the
storms of this life. If you lack internal direction,
trouble lies ahead.

The guidance you need comes only from the
Lord. In the words of the psalmist, *"I will praise
the Lord, who counsels me; even at night my heart
instructs me"* (Psalm 16:7).

"WRITE THE VISION"

Let me encourage you to write a personal
mission statement for your life. Make sure it
includes knowing the Lord, serving Him, living in

right relationships and using your gifts and talents to serve God, your family and the world around you.

After you clearly define your mission, take a moment to write detailed goals and objectives with specific timelines. What will you accomplish in ten years? Five years? One year? One month? One week? And what will you do tomorrow to move you closer to your dream?

God told the prophet Habakkuk, "*Write the vision, and make it plain upon tables, that he may run that readeth it*" (Habakkuk 2:2 KJV).

Do not get bogged down with the distractions of living which pull you away from your divine purpose. If 56 men were willing to sign a declaration which meant life or death, surely you can commit to a noble calling.

With God's help, stay true to your mission.

TAP INTO TRANSFORMING POWER

The reason our international television ministry is titled, "Touch the Fire" is because when we come in direct contact with the Spirit of God, our lives become bright flames which emanate His light to the world.

The same Jehovah who spoke to Moses through the burning bush desires to touch you today.

To discover the true secret of powerful people, pay attention to what Jesus said just before He ascended back to heaven: *"But ye shall receive power, after that the Holy Ghost is come upon you"* (Acts 1:8).

How did this power appear in the Upper Room? It came in the form of a *"fire"* that sat upon each of the 120 who had gathered (Acts 2:3).

It is an eternal torch, a beacon to the world which must never be extinguished. How do we keep it alive? Paul says, *"...fan into flame the gift of God, which is in you"* (2 Timothy 1:6).

I pray you will experience this heavenly fire.

Power In—More Power Out!

We can become strong by asking the Lord to multiply what we already possess.

We find this principle in the physical world by examining an electrical transformer. It can take low voltage and convert it into high voltage. However, it can't take "zero" power and turn it into something else. In other words, if you don't put power in, you won't get power out!

Thank God, He has given each of His children a certain amount of divine energy. We can either suppress it or ask the Lord to project and expand this Spirit-given resource.

The church is made up of people who possess the potential to change the world. But if this is to happen, we must place our energy into God's transformer—into His hands—so He can produce the results.

Remember, the Lord *"...is able to do exceeding abundantly above all that we ask or think, according to the power that worketh in us"* (Ephesians 3:20 KJV).

———————— ♦ ————————

What kind of power lies within you?
Is it dormant or active?

Most people don't have spiritual strength because they fail to touch the source. They lack abundance because they neglect to practice the law of the harvest by sowing into the Kingdom of God.

THE SPARK OF THE SPIRIT

An incredible amount of spiritual power is

135

available to you at this very moment. However, if you walk and think in the flesh, you *receive* in the flesh. But as you move in the Spirit you see, hear and receive God's resources *from* the Spirit.

Throughout Scripture there is a direct link between power and Spirit:

- Samson was able to tear a lion apart with his bare hands because *"...the Spirit of the Lord came upon him in power"* (Judges 14:6 NIV).
- Samuel declares, *"The Spirit of the Lord will come upon you in power...and you will be changed into a different person"* (1 Samuel 10:6).
- Paul says, "...through the power of the Spirit... I have fully proclaimed the gospel of Christ" (Romans 15:19).
- The Gospel comes to you, *"...not simply with words, but also with power, with the Holy Spirit and with deep conviction"* (1 Thessalonians 1:5).

YOUR HEAVENLY CONNECTION

Jesus is your OnStar®. When you need directions, just call on Him. When the doors are locked, connect with the Lord and allow Him to *"...open* [for] *you the windows of heaven, and pour you out a blessing, that there shall not be room enough to receive it"* (Malachi 3:10).

He is the Bright and Morning Star (Revelation 22:16). But you must have a "receiver" which He recognizes—a heart that has been washed in the cleansing blood of the Lamb.

Even better than OnStar®, God says, *"Before they call I will answer; while they are still speaking I will hear"* (Isaiah 65:24). And when you call He will *"...tell you great and unsearchable things you do not know"* (Jeremiah 33:3).

He is an on-time God!

"GREATER" THINGS

Before Jesus returned to heaven, He told us that

what He began on earth, we will finish —even more powerfully.

Jesus declared, *"I tell you the truth, anyone who has faith in me will do what I have been doing. He will do even greater things than these, because I am going to the Father"* (John 14:12).

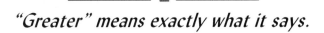

"Greater" means exactly what it says.

So when the Lord declares, *"...these signs will accompany those who believe"* (Mark 16:17), He is talking about you!

WISDOM, REVELATION, POWER

My prayer for you is found in the words of the apostle Paul: *"I have not stopped giving thanks for you, remembering you in my prayers. I keep asking that the God of our Lord Jesus Christ, the glorious Father, may give you the Spirit of wisdom and revelation, so that you may know him better. I pray also that the eyes of your heart may be enlightened in order that you may know the hope to which he has called you, the riches of his glorious inheritance in the saints, and his incomparably great power for us who believe"* (Ephesians 1:16-19).

Wisdom has worth, but when revelation is added to it, you experience transforming power.

It is God's desire that you become the strong, vibrant person He created you to be. Continue to tap into the secrets of powerful people revealed in His Word.

A glorious future is waiting just ahead!

NOTES

_____

_____

_____

_____

_____

_____

_____

_____

_____

_____

_____

_____

_____

_____

_____

_____

For a Complete List of Books, Tapes
and Other Materials, or to Schedule
the Author for Conferences, Seminars and
Speaking engagements, Contact:

Bishop H. Alan Mushegan
Gospel Harvester World Outreach Center
1521 Hurt Road
Marietta, GA 30008

Phone: 770-435-1152
Internet: www.gospelharvester.com